WHAT IT TAKES TO BE A PRO
BASEBALL PLAYER

by Joanne Mattern

STORY LIBRARY

MORE TO EXPLORE

www.12StoryLibrary.com

12-Story Library is an imprint of Bookstaves.

Photographs ©: Kyodo/Associated Press, cover, 1; Richard Wear/Alamy, 4; Keeton Gale/Shutterstock.com, 5; AS Food studio/Shutterstock.com, 6; Flavio Beltran/Shutterstock.com, 6; Eric Francis/Shutterstock.com, 7; John F. Shale/PD, 8; PD, 9; Bob Sandberg/Library of Congress, 9; Monkey Business Images/Shutterstock.com, 10; Photo Works/Shutterstock.com, 11; Joseph Sohm/Shutterstock.com, 12; Suzanne Tucker/Shutterstock.com, 13; Action Sports Photography/Shutterstock.com, 14; Frank Romeo/Shutterstock.com, 14; Aspen Photo/Shutterstock.com, 15; Aspen Photo/Shutterstock.com, 16; Jerry Zitterman/Shutterstock.com, 16; Aspen Photo/Shutterstock.com, 17; Action Sports Photography/Shutterstock.com, 18; Cheryl Ann Quigley/Shutterstock.com, 19; Library of Congress, 19; Fair Use, 20; Arturo Pardavila III/CC2.0, 20; Keith Allison/CC2.0, 21; PD, 22; Beyond My Ken/CC4.0, 23; Keith Allison/CC2.0, 24; Keith Allison/CC2.0, 25; Keith Allison/CC2.0, 26; PatersonGreatFalls/CC2.0, 27; George Grantham Bain/PD, 28; Library of Congress, 29

ISBN
9781632357595 (hardcover)
9781632358684 (paperback)
9781645820420 (ebook)

Library of Congress Control Number: 2019938631

Printed in the United States of America
July 2019

About the Cover
MLB All-Star Rhys Hoskins hits a home-run in the All-Star Series in 2018.

Access free, up-to-date content on this topic plus a full digital version of this book. Scan the QR code on page 31 or use your school's login at 12StoryLibrary.com.

Table of Contents

Life as a Baseball Pro: The Real Story

Players need to stretch every day.

For many people, playing professional baseball is a dream job. Maybe that's true for you. It would be wonderful to play in the major leagues. Maybe you could even be a big star.

It's fun to play a terrific sport and get paid for it. But playing professional baseball is also a very demanding job. Those lucky few who make it to the pros have to work hard.

All players exercise every day to keep their bodies strong and flexible. They don't get a break during the off-season, either. They have to train all year long. Training includes everything from running laps to lifting weights. Players even do yoga and Pilates to stay healthy.

In addition to training, players must follow rules set by their team. There are rules about how players should act and how they should look. Some teams, like the New York Yankees, forbid players from having facial hair except for mustaches. Some players refuse to play for the Yankees because of this rule. Other teams, like the

Bryce Harper (34) at bat for the Washington Nationals.

Houston Astros, sometimes make their players stay under a certain weight. And all teams forbid players, managers, or coaches to smoke or use chewing tobacco when they are on TV or around fans.

Travel is another rough part of baseball life. Pro players have games all over the country. Flying or traveling by bus can become boring. Players also spend a lot of time away from their families and friends.

Sure, being a pro baseball player is a great job. But it's not perfect.

10
Hours of sleep MLB outfielder Bryce Harper likes to get after a game

- Harper was the 2015 National League MVP.
- He lifts weights three days a week.
- After a game, he gets a massage of his feet and legs.

A Day in the Life

During the season, baseball players have a very busy life. A player might wake up late in the morning on a game day. He

probably eats a big breakfast, with lots of protein and fat to give him strength and energy.

Then it's off to the stadium for workouts. After an hour of weight lifting or other exercises, the player takes some swings in the batting cage. After a break for a late lunch, the team heads to the

field for more practice. It's time to stretch, run, and work on batting and fielding.

Many players enjoy a light dinner. Then they might play cards or video games. Other players listen to music or watch TV. But by early evening, it's time to get into uniform and take the field.

After the game, players might talk to the media. Others will get a massage and grab something to eat before going to bed. Morning and another day on the field will come quickly.

Players stay busy in the off-season, too. MLB left-fielder Matt Holliday drops his kids off at school. Then he heads for the gym and works out hard with a trainer. After that, he puts in some batting practice. He wants to be ready to play at the highest level possible when the next season starts.

187
Days in an MLB season

- Players report for spring training about six weeks before the season starts.
- The season begins in late March and runs until late September.
- Some players play in South American and Central American leagues during the off-season.

Staying in top shape is important for a pro baseball player.

A Brief History of the Game

Baseball is often called America's national pastime. And many people think of baseball as an American game. But baseball probably began in England more than 250 years ago. Back then, children played a game called rounders. Rounders was a lot like baseball. Players used a stick to hit a ball, then ran around bases to score. Colonists brought rounders to America when they came here from England.

In 1845, a group of men in New York formed a club. It was called the New York City Knickerbocker Baseball Club. One of them came up with rules for baseball that are still followed today.

Over the years, baseball became popular for all ages. Games were broadcast on the radio and later on TV. Heroes like Babe Ruth captured the attention of fans all over the nation. Leagues were formed and teams were added. In time, major league teams played from coast to coast.

Today baseball remains hugely popular. From local teams to school teams to the major leagues, baseball has fans of every age, gender, and color. The game is played in countries around the world.

A game of rounders in 1913.

The New York Knickerbockers in 1858.

1858

BASEBALL'S COLOR LINE

With very few exceptions in the late 1800s, African Americans were not allowed to play professional baseball. This wasn't an official rule. It's just how things were done. In 1945, Jackie Robinson signed a contract with the Brooklyn Dodgers. He played his first MLB game in 1947, breaking the color line.

1876
Year when the National League was formed

- The American League formed in 1901.
- The first World Series was played in 1903.
- In 2019, there were 30 Major League teams, 15 in each league.

4

Starting Young

If you want to be a professional baseball player, you have to start young. Children can start playing T-ball at ages three or four. By the time they are six or seven, they can move on to Little League.

Many MLB players took part in Little League when they were kids. Outfielder Aaron Judge dreamed of being a pro player from the time he was 10 years old. Center fielder Jackie Bradley Jr. didn't think a career in baseball was possible when he was a kid. He just loved to play, and baseball soon became the only thing he wanted to do.

In 2018, 27 percent of MLB players had been born in countries outside the United States. Many came from Central and South America or Japan. Baseball is very popular in these countries. First baseman Adrian Gonzalez, who grew up in Mexico, remembers playing baseball as a child. So did his older brothers and father. As long as you love the game, are good at it, and are willing to work hard, you can dream of a pro future.

Adrian Gonzalez at bat when he played for the San Diego Padres.

54

Current and former MLB players who played in the Little League World Series

- Brothers Cory and Colby Rasmus played in the 1999 Little League World Series.
- Colby is an outfielder. Cory is a pitcher.
- They later faced off against each other in the major leagues, when they played for different teams.

WHERE ARE THE WOMEN?

Girls have played Little League since 1974. But no women have ever played in Major League Baseball. Most girls who play baseball as kids switch to softball in high school and college. There are almost no opportunities for girls to play baseball as teenagers. This is a big reason why, so far, none has had a chance in MLB.

Beginning a Baseball Career

Outside of Little League, there are many opportunities for talented players to improve their skills. They can play on school teams in middle school, high school, and college. Playing in high school can be a great way for athletes to get better at the game. It is also a great way to get noticed.

College coaches are always looking for strong players. Many high-school athletes contact college coaches and send videos and other information about themselves. Coaches find players at baseball

244
Number of minor league baseball clubs

- About 6,500 athletes play on minor league teams. Only about 10 percent make it to the majors.
- About 1,200 athletes play on major league teams.
- There are five divisions in the minor leagues, from AAA (the highest level) to rookie teams (the lowest).

camps or special events called showcases. Some college coaches connect with high school athletic departments to find good players. Often, colleges will offer scholarships to encourage players to attend their schools.

Major league scouts are also on the lookout for young talent. Usually scouts recruit college players or find athletes at tryout camps. Major league teams hold a draft every year to choose players. It's unusual for a player to be drafted right out of high school, but it does happen. Shortstop and third baseman Alex Rodriguez ("A-Rod") was drafted by the Seattle Mariners in 1993. He was 18 and planning to go to college. Shortstop Derek Jeter was picked by the Yankees in 1992, right after high school.

THINK ABOUT IT

Do you think women will ever play professional baseball? What would have to change so women could join major league teams? Try to find out.

College coaches often visit baseball camps to find good players.

Staying in Top Shape

Baseball may look like an easy game to play compared with some other sports. However, professional baseball players are top athletes. They must be in great physical shape to play the game well.

There is a lot of running in baseball. Players must be able to run very quickly to get to base before they are tagged out. Players also need to change direction quickly and have good balance and agility. In addition, throwing and catching require physical strength and accuracy.

To stay in shape, serious players train every day. Exercises can include weight training to build strength in the arms, legs, and core. Players also run and box to stay fast and agile. Training can also include basic strength exercises like pushups, jumping jacks, and crunches.

Their brains have to be in top shape, too. Hitting a pitched ball takes lightning-fast thinking. Players have to decide in milliseconds whether to swing, how hard, and where to aim the bat.

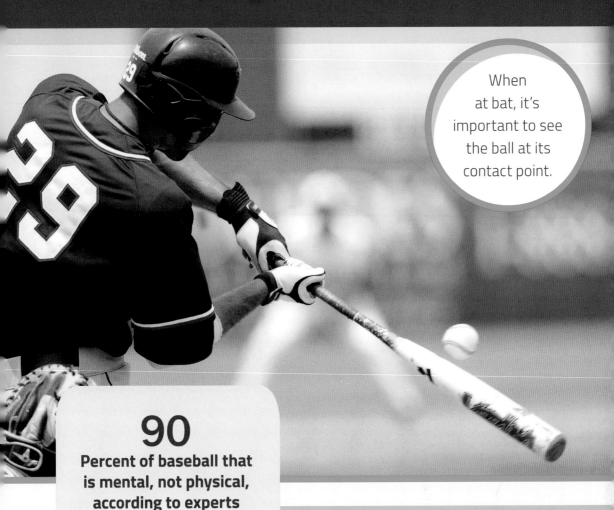

When at bat, it's important to see the ball at its contact point.

90

Percent of baseball that is mental, not physical, according to experts

- Hall of Famer Yogi Berra and major league manager Charlie Manuel both said this at different times.
- Players like shortstop Derek Jeter mentally picture themselves hitting the ball or making the catch.
- Pros don't think about a missed catch or a strikeout. They focus on the moment.

EYE ON THE BALL

Hitting a baseball is said to be one of the most difficult things to do in sports. Many great players have excellent eyesight. For the average person, 20/20 is perfect vision. Baseball pros often have 20/12 vision. This means they can see something 20 feet away that most people have to be 12 feet away to see.

Taking a Risk

Baseball can be tough on a person's body. For most players, injuries are a part of life. Sprains and pulled muscles are the most common. These injuries usually aren't serious and can be treated with ice, heat, and rest.

How can baseball players stay healthy? Stretching is key. Players should warm up before training or playing and cool down afterward. Warm-ups and cool-downs help loosen muscles so there is less chance of injury. Stretching helps muscles feel less sore.

Knee injuries are also common and can be serious. Sometimes a player twists his knee sliding into base. Or he may injure it if he stops suddenly or changes direction. These movements can tear ligaments in the knee. These injuries are often very painful. Major injuries can need surgery to be fixed. Minor injuries will heal with rest and physical therapy.

Swinging a baseball bat over and over can injure the lower back. Usually, resting and physical therapy can heal these injuries. More serious injuries might need surgery.

Warming up and stretching before playing prevents injury.

198

Number of injuries that put players on the disabled list (DL) in 2015

- Elbow injuries were the most common.
- MLB players spent a total of 30,000 days on the DL in 2015.
- In 2019, MLB renamed the disabled list the injured list. Advocates for people with disabilities wanted them to make this change.

PITCHING PROBLEMS

Most baseball injuries happen to pitchers. In March 2017, 45 of the 60 players on the DL were pitchers. Doctors say most of these injuries are caused by overuse. Throwing a ball 90 miles an hour—or even faster—over and over causes a lot of damage to a pitcher's elbow and shoulder. Doctors warn younger players not to pitch for long periods of time and to get plenty of rest between games. This can prevent problems that could end a major league career before it starts.

Pitcher Jhonathan Ramos (36) in 2014.

8

Putting on the Gear

Compared to athletes in other sports, most baseball players don't wear a lot of equipment. Players in the field just wear a uniform, a glove, and a hat to keep the sun out of their eyes.

All fielders wear gloves. These gloves are made of leather and have a webbed pocket to hold the ball. Gloves not only make the ball easier to catch, they also protect the player's hand from injuries. If a player is right-handed, he wears the glove on his left hand. This allows him to throw the ball with the hand that isn't wearing the glove.

Batters also wear gloves to protect their hands from blisters from swinging the bat. All players wear cleats, or spiked shoes, for a better grip on the ground when they run.

Catchers wear the most equipment. Pitches are thrown at them and players swing bats right in front of them. A catcher wears a face mask and a helmet, a chest protector, and shin guards. Because catchers spend most of their time crouching, some wear knee savers. These are special pads worn on the legs to help a player rest his knees.

1929

Year when MLB teams started putting numbers on uniforms

- The New York Yankees had the idea first, but their opening game was rained out.
- The Cleveland Indians became the first team to use numbers.
- Jackie Robinson's number, 42, was retired in 1997 to honor this baseball great.

BATTING HELMETS SAVE LIVES

Today all baseball players wear helmets to protect their heads when they are up at bat. That wasn't the case in 1920, when shortstop Ray Chapman was hit in the head by a pitch. He died a few hours later. Batting helmets weren't required until 1941. To date, Chapman is the only major league player killed during a game.

Baseball Honors

Major league players are great, but some are the best of the best. During every season, MLB gives awards to the best players.

The All-Star Game is usually played in July and features players from each major league team. The public and the players choose the players by voting. After the game, one player is named the Most Valuable Player, or MVP.

As of 2018, 45 of the 195 MVPs were from California. Why so many? One reason is because California has more people than any other state. Another reason is its weather. You can grow up there playing baseball year-round. What state has

The 2019 All-Star Game was at Progressive Field in Cleveland.

25

Times Hank Aaron appeared in All-Star Games

- The first All-Star Game was played in 1933.
- Babe Ruth hit the first home run in an All-Star Game.
- Between 1959 and 1962, there were two All-Star Games each season.

J.J. Hardy and Adam Jones receive Gold Glove Awards.

the fewest MVPs?

Until 2018, Tennessee had none. Then outfielder Mookie Betts, a Nashville native, won the award.

Most awards are given out after the season ends. The Baseball Writers of America choose an MVP from the American League and the National League. The Baseball Writers also choose the Manager of the Year, the Rookie of the Year, and the Cy Young Award for each league. The Cy Young Award goes to the best pitcher.

MLB also gives out awards to fielders and hitters. One fielder at each position in each league wins a Gold Glove Award. The best hitters from each team win the Silver Slugger Award. Awards are also given to relievers and designated hitters.

Going to Cooperstown

For baseball players, there is no greater honor than being elected to the National Baseball Hall of Fame. The Hall of Fame started in 1936. The first players to be inducted were Ty Cobb, Babe Ruth, Honus Wagner, Christy Mathewson, and Walter Johnson.

games, autograph signings, speeches, and other events.

Players aren't the only members of the Hall of Fame. Managers, umpires, executives, and broadcasters can also be elected. Members are chosen by the Baseball

Left to right: Cobb, Ruth, Wagner, Mathewson, and Johnson.

In 1939, the Hall of Fame museum opened in Cooperstown, New York. Every year since then, baseball's best players are inducted during a weekend filled with baseball

Writers of America. A player must have played for at least 10 years and be retired for 5 years to be considered for the Hall.

It isn't easy to get into the Hall of Fame. The odds are about 70 to 1.

The National Baseball Hall of Fame in Cooperstown, New York.

It's even harder to get in on the first try. Only 1 in 7 players were chosen the first time they were eligible. In 2018, pitcher Mariano Rivera became the first person elected unanimously.

THINK ABOUT IT

What would it feel like to be elected to the Hall of Fame? Do some research to find out what players think about this honor.

300,000
People who visit the Hall of Fame each year

- The Hall of Fame Library has more than 3 million documents.
- The Library has a file for everyone who played in a major league game.
- The Library also has 250,000 photographs and 14,000 hours of film.

After the Game

Even the best baseball player can't play forever. The average career of a major league player is just 5½ years. One in five players only plays for a year. Some might go up and down between the major leagues and the minor leagues. And many players never get out of the minor leagues at all.

Once a baseball player's career on the field is over, there are other jobs he can do. Some players become managers of a major league or minor league team. First baseman Don Mattingly played for the New York Yankees for 14 years and won many awards. After he retired, he managed the Los Angeles Dodgers between 2011 and 2015. Then he moved on to manage the Miami Marlins.

Other former players go into broadcasting. Shortstop and third baseman Cal Ripken Jr., who holds the record for most games played in a row, went into the broadcast booth after he retired. Still others work for a team's business office or even become an owner. Shortstop Derek Jeter became part of a group that bought the Miami Marlins in 2017. He also took a position as the team's head of operations.

First baseman Don Mattingly went on to coaching after playing the game.

WORKING OUTSIDE OF BASEBALL

Some former MLB players go on to jobs that have nothing to do with sports. Pitcher Byung-hyun Kim opened a sushi restaurant. Second baseman Adrian Cárdenas became a writer. Relief pitcher Mark Wohlers went into real estate. The tag line for his business is "We go to bat for you!"

45

Age in years of pitcher Bartolo Colon, the oldest active player in baseball in 2018

- Colon was born in the Dominican Republic. His father taught him to play baseball.
- He lied about his age, saying he was 18 when he signed with the Cleveland Indians in 1993. He was actually 20.
- Colon has played for 11 different teams over his long career.

Cal Ripken Jr. (left) with Ernie Johnson Jr. in the broadcast booth.

Doing Good and Giving Back

Baseball players can be heroes on the field. They can be heroes off the field as well. Many players take part in charity work. They do a lot to give back to their community and to people in need.

Designated hitter and first basemen David Ortiz was known as "Big Papi" when he played for the Boston Red Sox. In 2005, Ortiz visited a children's hospital and decided to start the David Ortiz Children's Fund. The Fund has helped children in New England and also in Ortiz's home country of the Dominican Republic.

Shortstop and third baseman Cal Ripken Jr. also loves to help children. His goal is to use baseball to teach life lessons to young people living in difficult conditions. Ripken and his brother have opened several youth baseball complexes. They run a foundation named after their father, who was also a major league baseball star.

David Ortiz (left) and the Baltimore Orioles support the World Pediatric Project.

Pitcher Mariano Rivera was elected to the Baseball Hall of Fame in 2018, but he was already a star in the eyes of children around the world. Rivera

17

Years Roberto Clemente played in the major leagues

- Clemente, a right fielder, had 3,000 hits during his years with the Pittsburgh Pirates.
- In 1972, he flew to Nicaragua to donate supplies after an earthquake. His plane crashed and he was killed.
- Each year since 1971, MLB has given the Roberto Clemente Award to a player who best demonstrates community involvement.

THINK ABOUT IT

Does it matter if professional athletes give back? Why or why not?

is another player who believes in helping children who are poor or who live in struggling communities. His foundation focuses on school, sports, and community.

Roberto Clemente's legacy continues to help children today.

27

Fun Facts about Baseball

- Legend says that baseball was invented by Abner Doubleday in Cooperstown, New York, in 1839. Abner Doubleday was a real person, but the story was not true. It was made up by a man named A.G. Spalding. Spalding wanted people to believe that baseball was a completely American game.

- Every pro game starts with a ceremonial first pitch. This tradition began with President William Howard Taft in 1910. At that same game, Taft also started the tradition of the seventh-inning stretch. He got up to stretch in the middle of the seventh inning and the crowd did, too.

- If a pitcher is throwing a no-hitter or a perfect game, superstition says no one can talk to him about it until the game is over.

- What can a fan do to help his or her team win? Wear a rally cap. Fans turn their caps inside-out to bring the team good luck when they need it most.

A. G. Spalding was a major league baseball pitcher who played between 1871 and 1878.

President Taft at the 1910 game.

- If a team doesn't win the World Series for many years, many fans believe the team is cursed. After selling Babe Ruth's contract to the New York Yankees in 1919, the Boston Red Sox didn't win the World Series until 2004, 85 years later. Fans called this the Curse of the Bambino. During a World Series game in 1945, the Chicago Cubs refused to let a man enter the ballpark with his pet goat. The man cursed the team, saying they would never win a World Series. The Curse of the Billy Goat lasted for 71 years. The Cubs finally won the Series in 2016.

- It's against the rules for a player to catch a ball in his hat or throw his hat or glove at the ball to knock it down. If a player does this, the batter scores three runs.

- If a ball gets stuck in the catcher's face mask, all the runners get to advance one base.

Glossary

agility
The ability to move quickly and easily.

broadcast
To transmit something on radio or TV.

core
In anatomy, the muscles of the back and abdomen.

draft
A procedure where teams select new players.

foundation
An organization that gives money to charity.

inducted
Admitted to an organization.

league
A group of sports clubs.

recruit
To ask someone to join a team or organization.

relievers
Pitchers who enter the game in place of a previous pitcher.

scholarship
Money paid to support a student's education.

scouts
People who look for talented players to add to a team.

unanimous
Agreed on by everyone.

Read More

Aretha, David. *Top 10 Moments in Baseball.* New York: Enslow Publishing, 2016.

Burgan, Michael. *Breaking Barriers: The Story of Jackie Robinson.* North Mankato, MN: Capstone Press, 2018.

Luke, Andrew. *Baseball.* Broomall, PA: Mason Crest, 2017.

Osborne, Mary Pope, and Natalie Pope Boyce. *Baseball. Magic Tree House Fact Tracker.* New York: Random House Children's Books, 2017.

Pina, Andrew. *Becoming a Pro Baseball Player.* New York: Gareth Stevens, 2015.

Visit 12StoryLibrary.com

Scan the code or use your school's login at **12StoryLibrary.com** for recent updates about this topic and a full digital version of this book. Enjoy free access to:

- Digital ebook
- Breaking news updates
- Live content feeds
- Videos, interactive maps, and graphics
- Additional web resources

Note to educators: Visit 12StoryLibrary.com/register to sign up for free premium website access. Enjoy live content plus a full digital version of every 12-Story Library book you own for every student at your school.

Index

About the Author

Joanne Mattern has been writing books for children for more than 25 years. She loves to write about sports and has been a baseball fan all her life. Joanne lives in New York State with her family.

READ MORE FROM 12-STORY LIBRARY

Every 12-Story Library Book is available in many fomats. For more information, visit **12StoryLibrary.com**